Instant Bible Lessons® for toddlers

Growing Up for God

Mary J. Davis

These pages may be copied.

Permission is granted to the buyer of this book to
photocopy student materials for use with
Sunday school or Bible teaching classes.

An imprint of Rose Publishing, Inc.
Carson, CA
www.Rose-Publishing.com

To Brandi and Amanda, two young ladies who serve the Lord above and beyond, always. Your example is a wonderful one for adults and young people alike.

To Karl and Yvonne, dear friends.

To Larry, Jeff and Pam, Wendi, Lori.

INSTANT BIBLE LESSONS® FOR TODDLERS: GROWING UP FOR GOD
©2014 BY MARY J. DAVIS, fourteenth printing
ISBN 10: 1-58411-037-6
ISBN 13: 978-1-58411-037-8
RoseKidz® reorder# R38212
RELIGION / CHRISTIAN MINISTRY / CHILDREN

RoseKidz®
AN IMPRINT OF ROSE PUBLISHING, INC.
17909 ADRIA MARU LANE
CARSON, CA 90746
WWW.ROSE-PUBLISHING.COM

Cover and Interior Illustrator: Mary Rojas

Scriptures are from the *Holy Bible: New International Version* (North American Edition), ©1973, 1978, 1984 by the International Bible Society. Used by permission of Zondervan Bible Publishers.

Printed in China

▪▫▪ Contents ▪▫▪

continued on page 4...

Chapter 9: More Ways to Grow for God 88

■ ● ■ Introduction ■ ● ■

Do your toddlers know how God wants them to grow up? Knowing that God expects certain things for us is a first step in wanting to live our lives for God. After they participate in the activities in *Growing Up for God*, toddlers will know that God wants us to be kind, helpful, loving, thankful, sharing, healthy, obedient and a good friend to others. Toddlers will want to be what God wants them to be!

Each of the first eight chapters includes a Bible story, memory verse and a variety of activities to help reinforce the truth in the lesson. An additional chapter contains miscellaneous projects that can be used anytime throughout the study, or at the end to review the lessons.

The most exciting aspect of *Instant Bible Lessons for Toddlers*, which includes *Jesus Is My Friend*, *God Blesses Me* and *God Takes Care of Me*, is its flexibility. You can easily adapt these lessons to a Sunday school hour, a children's church service, a Wednesday night Bible study or family home use. And because there is a variety of reproducible ideas from which to choose (see below), you will enjoy creating a class session that is best for your group of students, whether large or small, beginning or advanced, active or studious. The intriguing topics will keep your kids coming back for more, week after week.

With these lessons, toddlers will learn what kind of person God wants them to be. They will want to grow up with God!

✳ How to Use This Book ✳

Each chapter begins with a Bible story which you may read to your class in one of two levels, followed by discussion questions. Following each story page is a story visual for you to make and use as you tell the story. Every story chapter also includes a bulletin board poster with the memory verse and suggestions for using the poster as an activity. All of the activities are tagged with one of the icons below, so you can quickly flip through the chapter and select the projects you need. Simply cut off the teacher instructions on the pages and duplicate!

craft   teacher help   story visual   action verse   bulletin board   activity

puzzle   coloring   song   game   snack

Chapter 1

God Wants Me to Be Kind

Memory Verse

What I have I give you. Acts 3:6

* Story to Share *

2's and 3's →

One day, Peter and John were going to the temple to pray. They saw a man who was being carried to the temple gate. The man asked for money there every day.

This man had never been able to walk. He asked people for money so he could buy food and other things he needed.

When the man saw Peter and John, he asked them for money.

"We have no silver or gold," Peter said. "But what I have, I give to you."

God had given Peter the power to make people well. Peter said to the man, "In the name of Jesus Christ of Nazareth, get up and walk." Peter took the man's hand and helped him stand up. Instantly, the man's feet and ankles became strong.

The man began to jump and shout, "Praise God. He has made me well."

All the people who saw this man were filled with wonder and amazement. They knew something very special had happened to the man.

1's and young 2's

A man was not able to walk. He sat at the gate of the temple every day to ask people for money. One day, he asked Peter and John for money. Peter said, "I don't have money, but I can give you something else." Peter said, "In the name of Jesus, get up and walk."

Peter helped the man to his feet. The man was so happy to be able to walk that he went away jumping and shouting. He told everyone that God had made him well.

Based on Acts 3:1-10

Questions for Discussion

1. Why did the man ask for money?

2. What did Peter do for the man?

story visual

• • • • • • • • • • •

What You Need
• duplicated page
• Bulletin Board
  Poster, page 10

What to Do
1. Cut out and color
   the Bendable Man.
2. Fold the man on
   the dashed lines so
   the man will sit or
   stand.
3. To tell the story,
   fold the man so he
   is sitting as you
   begin the story.
   Show the bulletin
   board poster. Stand
   up the Bendable
   Man as the story
   progresses. Make
   him leap and walk!

Another Idea
Show the children
what it would be like
to not be able to walk.
Sit the children in a
circle. Sit in a chair
inside the circle. Offer
the children a cookie,
but tell them they
cannot use their legs
to reach the cookie.

■ **Kind** ■

• Bendable Man •

fold
fold

**finished
visual**

8

• Bulletin Board Poster •

Poster Pointer

Fasten the poster onto a bulletin board in your classroom. To make it stand out, mount it onto brightly-colored construction paper, leaving an edge of the construction paper showing. Color the poster with crayons or markers.

bulletin board

. . . .

What You Need
- pattern on page 10
- construction paper or card stock
- clear, self-stick plastic
- glue
- tape
- yarn

What to Do
1. Depending on how you want to use the poster (see ideas below and at left), enlarge, reduce or simply copy page 10 to fit your bulletin board space.
2. To use the poster as an in-class activity, show how to make a Scripture windsock. Glue the poster to a sheet of construction paper. Roll the construction paper into a tube and tape the seam. Tape several 1" x 11" strips of construction paper to the bottom edge of the windsock. Tape a length of yarn to the top of the windsock for a hanger.

■ Kind ■

What I have I give you.
Acts 3:6

• Folding Picture •

What You Need
• duplicated page
• crayons

What to Do
1. Allow the children to color the pictures.
2. Help the children fold the illustration on the dashed lines so they meet, hiding the healed man.
3. As you read the story, show how to open the flap to see the man after he was healed.

Peter and John went to pray at the temple.
A crippled man begged for money.
Peter said, "I'm sorry. Money I do not have.
But maybe you'd like something better."

The crippled man didn't know what Peter meant.
But then Peter said, "Get up."
He held out his hand to help the man.
And then, the crippled man could walk!

(Acts 3:1-10)

■ **Kind** ■

11

verse/song

What You Need

• duplicated page

What to Do

1. Before class, practice saying "Be Kind" and singing "Peter Was Very Kind" with the movements.
2. As you lead the children in saying "Be Kind," encourage them to leap and wave their arms. Stress that the man was very happy to be able to use his legs.
3. Sing "Peter Was Very Kind" to the tune of "London Bridge" using the action movements as shown.

■ Kind ■

• Be Kind •

Be Kind

Peter healed the crippled man.
He made his legs all well.
The man went away leaping and shouting
For the good news he wanted to tell.

Peter was kind to the crippled man.
And the man went on his way.
God wants us to be kind to others.
We can learn to be kind every day.

Peter Was Very Kind

The crippled man sat on the street,
On the street,
On the street.
The crippled man sat on the street,
And he said, "Please be kind."

sit down

Peter and John he did meet,
He did meet,
He did meet.
Peter and John he did meet,
And he said, "Please be kind."

*pretend to shake hands
with someone*

Peter healed that man's feet,
That man's feet,
That man's feet.
Peter healed that man's feet.
Peter was very kind.

touch feet

The man could walk and he praised God,
He praised God,
He praised God.
The man could walk and he praised God,
Because Peter was very kind.

pretend to walk and run

• Be Kind Flower •

God

Wants

Me

to

Be

Kind.

(Acts 3:1-10)

craft

What You Need
• duplicated page
• paper plate
• glue
• crayons

What to Do
1. Before class, cut out the six flower petals for each child.
2. Help the children glue the flower petals around the edge of the plate.
3. Say, **Our flower says, "God wants me to be kind." Can you tell some ways to be kind?**

■ **Kind** ■

13

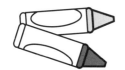

coloring

. . . .

What You Need
- duplicated page
- crayons

What to Do
1. Hold a copy of the page so that the children can see it as you tell the life application story.
2. Afterward, while the children color their pictures, ask, **Can you name some other ways we can be kind?**

• Lots of Puppies & Kittens •

"Look at that," Dad said. "The television news says they need help at the animal shelter. They have lots of dogs and cats who need to be fed and cared for."

"Oh, I want to go see the puppies," Nathan said. "I can help feed the puppies."

Meg said. "Dad, I can help, too." Nathan knew his big sister loved cats. But Nathan loved puppies.

"Well," Dad said. "I guess we have a project, then. I'll call the shelter and tell them we can help on Saturdays."

Saturday came, and Nathan was out of bed early. He couldn't wait to go see all the puppies.

When they arrived at the pet shelter, Nathan was the first one inside. "I came to see the puppies," he said.

Dad and Meg came into the building. "My son loves puppies," Dad said. "And my daughter loves cats."

"Well, that will work out just fine," the caretaker said. "Follow me. I have a good job for each of you."

They followed the man into a large room. Nathan couldn't believe his eyes. There were cages and cages with big dogs, little dogs, puppies, kittens and cats. The man gave Nathan some puppy food. He gave Dad some food for the bigger dogs. And, of course, Meg got to feed the cats.

Nathan played with the puppies while he fed them. He sat on the floor and let the puppies crawl on him.

"You are very kind to puppies," the caretaker said. "I would like to have you come help us again."

Dad nodded. "God wants you to be kind," Dad said. "You can be kind every Saturday by helping to feed the puppies."

■ Kind ■

14

• Kindness Bee Bowling •

pin diagram

game

What You Need
- duplicated page
- 10 toilet tissue tubes
- tape
- sponge

What to Do
1. Before class, make the bowling pins by coloring and cutting out the 10 bees. Tape one to each of the tissue tubes. If you have a large class, make several sets of pins.
2. Stand the bowling pins in a V-shaped pattern (rows of 1, 2, 3 and 4 pins).
3. Have the children stand back from the pins a bit. They should toss the sponge at the bowling pins to knock them down.
4. Say, **These little bees remind us that God wants us to BEE kind. We can be kind by taking turns playing our game.**

■ Kind ■

game

What You Need

- rope
- hula hoop
- riding toys that use legs to push
- soft mat to jump on
- wheelchair

What to Do

1. Let the children jump over a rope held by two adults an inch off the ground. Have them jump in and out of an upright hula hoop that is laying on the floor and through another hula hoop that is held upright at ground level. Hold some riding toy races. Have the children jump up and down on the soft mat.

2. After they do these things, have the children take turns riding in the wheelchair.

3. Say, **It's not easy to play without our legs, is it? The man in our story couldn't run or jump or even walk. Peter was kind to that man. Peter healed the man's legs. God wants us to be kind.**

■ Kind ■

• Using Our Legs •

Chapter 2

God Wants Me to Be Helpful

Memory Verse

Dorcas [Tabitha]....was always doing good and helping the poor. **Acts 9:36**

✻ Story to Share ✻

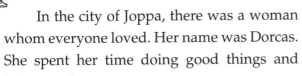

2's and 3's ⟶

In the city of Joppa, there was a woman whom everyone loved. Her name was Dorcas. She spent her time doing good things and helping others.

One day, Dorcas got very sick, and she died. Her friends cried and were very sad. They sent for Peter, who was in another city. God had given Peter the power to make people well. The people wanted Peter to bring Dorcas back to life.

Peter went into the room where Dorcas lay. Many people were crying and telling Peter about the good things Dorcas had done for them. She helped a lot of people. She helped people by making clothes for them.

Peter sent all the people out of the room. He took Dorcas by the hand. "Get up," he said. Peter helped Dorcas get up. Then, he called all her friends back into the room.

All her friends were happy that she was alive. They told many people what had happened.

1's and young 2's ⟶

Dorcas was a woman who helped people. One day, she became sick and died. But her friends wanted Peter to bring her back to life again. God had given him this special power.

Peter came into the room where all the people were crying. They showed Peter some clothes that Dorcas had made for them.

Peter took Dorcas' hand and helped her up. She was alive again. Her friends were happy.

Based on Acts 9:36-43

Questions for Discussion

1. Why did the people love Dorcas?

2. What did Peter do to help Dorcas and the people?

story visual

What You Need

- this page and page 19, duplicated
- craft sticks
- 6.5" x 10" piece of 1-inch thick foam
- craft knife

What to Do

1. Glue the scene from page 19 onto the foam.
2. Use a craft knife to cut slits in the page through the foam where indicated.
3. Color and cut out the figures and tape each one to a craft stick.
4. To tell the story, place the scene board on a table. As you tell the story, stick the figures with craft sticks in the slits in the scene. Lie the woman on the bed to start. Place Peter at the end of the bed. Then have the woman sit and then stand beside bed. Groups of people will be in the room for part of the story, leave and then come back.

■ Helpful ■

• Stand-up Story •

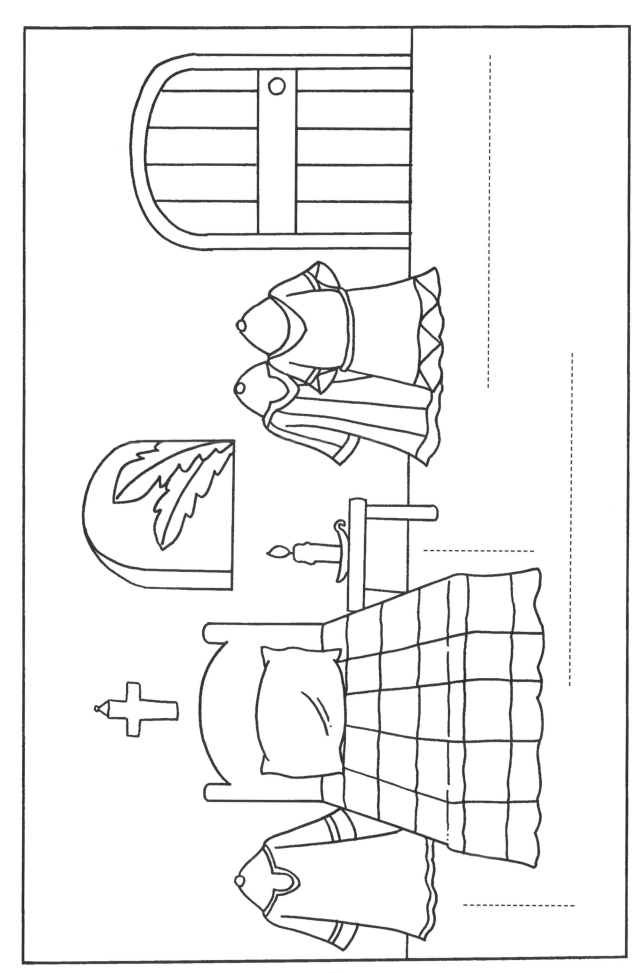

bulletin board

. . . .

What You Need
• pattern on page 21
• construction paper or card stock
• clear, self-stick plastic
• paper grocery bags

What to Do
1. Depending on how you want to use the poster (see ideas below and at right), enlarge, reduce or simply copy page 21 to fit your bulletin board space.
2. To use the poster as an in-class activity, make a food collection bag. Copy the page for each child. Glue the page to the side of a brown grocery bag. Have the children take their bags home, perhaps with a note to parents to collect canned food items and return them to class. Give the items to a needy family or a food pantry.

■ **Helpful** ■

• Bulletin Board Poster •

Poster Pointer

Copy the poster onto card stock for stability. Use colored card stock for effect. Attach the posters onto the wall at the children's eye level to use in review. Or, attach the posters to the wall outside your classroom so parents will be familiar with the lessons the children are learning.

**Dorcas...was always doing good
and helping the poor.**
Acts 9:36

• Dot-to-dot Dorcas •

puzzle

What You Need
- duplicated page
- crayons

What to Do
1. Help the children complete the dot-to-dot picture.
2. Say, **I wonder who is giving the people new clothes. Yes, it's Dorcas. Dorcas helped many people.**
3. Read the story to the children.

Many people in Joppa were poor. They didn't have enough money to buy clothes or food. But someone in Joppa was very good to the poor people. It was Dorcas! Dorcas helped others all the time.

One day, Dorcas got sick and died. Her friends sent for Peter. They knew he could help them because God had given him a special power. Peter came to the house. He sent all the people out of the room where Dorcas was. Peter said, "Dorcas, get up." He held out his hand and helped her get up.

The people were very happy that Dorcas was alive again. They told everyone what Peter had done.

Dorcas was a helper. People loved her very much. She helped people because God said it is the right thing to do. God wants us to be helpful.

■ Helpful ■

• Dorcas Liked to Help •

Dorcas Liked to Help

Dorcas liked to help.
Dorcas liked to help.
She helped lots of people.
Dorcas liked to help.

God wants me to help.
God wants me to help.
I can help other people,
God wants me to help.

Helping

I help you.

point to others

You help me.

point to self

That's the way God wants us to be.

point to God

song/verse

What You Need
- duplicated page
- cloth or sponge

What to Do
1. While the children sing "Dorcas Liked to Help" with you to the tune of "The Farmer in the Dell" encourage them to pretend to dust or wash the floor or table with a cloth or sponge.
2. Do the "Helping" rhyme slowly with the easy actions. For older children, say the rhyme several times, going faster each time for added fun.

■ Helpful ■

craft

What You Need

- duplicated page
- gallon plastic milk jugs (one per child)
- tape
- string

What to Do

1. Before class, remove and discard the caps from the jugs. Cut a hole in the front of each jug as shown in the illustration. Leave the handle intact. Cut the label from the duplicated page for each child.
2. Allow the children to color the label.
3. Go around and write each child's name on his or her label.
4. Help the children tape the label onto the milk jug, just below the cut off portion.
5. Show how to hold the Pick-up Bucket and put toys or crayons inside, then carry the items to be put away.
6. Say, **You can use your Pick-up Bucket to help put away your toys and books at home. God wants us to be helpful.**

■ Helpful ■

• Pick-up Buckets •

's Pick-up Bucket

Acts 9:36

how to cut

• Helping a New Friend •

puzzle

What You Need
• duplicated page
• crayons

What to Do
1. Hold a copy of the page for all the children to see as you read the story.
2. Afterward, give each child a copy of the page. Help the children find the hidden objects.
3. Say, **Can you help find the toys? Color the toys when you find them. Mandy helped her new friend. How can you help a friend? God wants us to be helpful.**

"Look!" Mandy said. "There's a big truck outside."

Mandy's mom looked out the window. "Oh, it's a moving truck. A family is moving into the blue house across the street. We should do something to help. Let's watch and see if the family is there yet."

Mandy watched the movers carry many boxes inside the house. She saw them carry a sofa, a big table and some beds.

"I see some children," Mom said. "Look over by the garage."

Mandy was glad to see children. There were three children. One was a boy about her age.

"What can we do to help?" Mandy asked.

Mom brought out a big plate of sandwich meat. "I'll wrap this up, and you can carry a loaf of bread." Mandy and Mom went across the street.

"Hello," Mom said to the children. A woman walked out of the house.

"We are the Smiths," the woman said. "My children were hoping to have new friends here. I am glad to see you have a girl their age."

Mandy handed the loaf of bread to Mrs. Smith. The little boy came to her and said, "We have a new toy room. Do you want to come inside and see it?"

Mandy followed her new friend. She helped him put away toys. It was fun to help. It was fun to make a new friend.

• Helpful •

25

snack

What You Need
- pudding
- candy sprinkles
- shaker container
- paper cups
- plastic spoons
- napkins

What to Do
1. Have plenty of adult helpers. Place bowls of one or more flavors of pudding on the table where the children can easily reach it.
2. Place a shaker filled with candy sprinkles on the table.
3. Say, **I need help making this snack. Will you help me?** While the adult holds a cup, have the child spoon in some pudding.
4. Then have the children help shake on some sprinkles over the pudding. Say, **You did a great job helping me.** Then pray, **Thank You, God, for this snack and for this helpful class. Amen.** Enjoy!

▪ Helpful ▪

• Helper Sundaes •

• Helping Cloths •

_____'s Helping Cloth

God wants me to be helpful.

(Acts 9:36-43)

craft

What You Need
- duplicated page
- cheesecloth or other soft cloth
- tape

What to Do
1. Before class, cut the cloth into 6-inch squares, one per child.
2. Cut out the envelope and give each child an envelope and a square of cloth.
3. Help the children fold the figure on the dashed lines to form an envelope. Tape the envelope closed.
4. Help the children place their helping cloths inside the envelope.
5. Say, **When you go home, you can dust a table with your helping cloth. God wants us to be helpers.**
6. Show how to dust the table with the helping cloth.

▪ Helpful ▪

Chapter 3

God Wants Me to Be Loving

Memory Verse

Love the Lord…and love your neighbor. Luke 10:27

* Story to Share *

2's and 3's ➝

A man asked Jesus, "What do I need to do to live with You in heaven?" Jesus said, "What is written in God's Word? You should know."

The man knew. He answered. "It says, 'Love the Lord your God with all your heart…and love your neighbor.'"

Jesus said, "That is right. That's what God wants you to do."

The man asked another question. "Who is my neighbor?" So Jesus told a story. He said a man was traveling. Some robbers beat him up and stole his money. They left him on the road. Two men from the man's own country came by and wouldn't stop to help him. Then a Samaritan came along. He was from another country. It was unusual for people from the two places to help each other. But, the Samaritan couldn't leave the injured man there to die. He put bandages on the man and then took him on a donkey to an inn. He took good care of the injured man.

Jesus asked, "Which of these three men do you think was a neighbor to the injured man?"

Of course, the answer was, "The Samaritan, who helped the hurt man."

1's and young 2's ➝

A man asked Jesus, "What does God want me to do?" Jesus asked, "What does God's Word say?" The man answered, "Love the Lord your God and love your neighbor."

"That is right," Jesus said.

The man asked, "Who is my neighbor?" Jesus told a story about a good neighbor. A man was beaten and robbed and left in the road. Two men came by and wouldn't help. But then, a man from far away stopped and helped. "Who was a good neighbor?" Jesus asked. The good neighbor was the man who helped.

Based on Luke 10:25-37

? Questions for Discussion

1. What does God's Word say for us to do?

2. Why was the Samaritan a good neighbor?

• Stand-up Story Triangle •

story visual
. . . .

What You Need
- duplicated page
- tape

What to Do
1. Color the pictures.
2. Fold the stand-up story triangle on the dashed lines.
3. Tape at the seam.
4. To tell the story, place the stand-up story triangle on the table. Turn the triangle to the various scenes as you tell the story.

More Ideas
1. Invite another class for a snack. Say, **We can love our neighbors by inviting them for a party.**
2. Duplicate the Stand-up Story Triangle for each child. Help the children fold the triangle and tape at the seam. Show how to turn the triangle to show the story scenes.

■ Loving ■

bulletin board

What You Need
- pattern on page 31
- construction paper or card stock
- clear, self-stick plastic
- crayons
- envelopes

What to Do

1. Depending on how you want to use the poster (see ideas below and at right), enlarge, reduce or simply copy page 31 to fit your bulletin board space.

2. To use the poster as an in-class activity, make a puzzle. Give each child a copy of the poster and have them color the picture. Then cut the scene into three or four pieces. Help the children assemble their puzzles. Provide an envelope for each child to carry the puzzle home.

■ Loving ■

• Bulletin Board Poster •

Poster Pointer

Make the poster durable by covering it with clear, self-stick plastic. Let each child hold a covered poster. While the children are holding the posters, say the memory verse together several times.

Love the Lord...And love your neighbor.
Luke 10:27

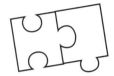

puzzle

What You Need
- duplicated page
- crayons

What to Do
1. Have the children point to each picture scene while you read the corresponding story phrase.
2. Have the children color their pictures.
3. Help the children connect the dots to make a heart around the final part of the story.
4. Say, **Let's find the heart on the page. There it is. The heart reminds us to love God and love each other. The Samaritan man showed love by helping the man who was hurt.**

• Showing Love •

God's Word says, "Love the Lord your God…and love your neighbor." A man asked Jesus, "Who is my neighbor?" Jesus told this story.

A man was robbed and beaten. He was left on the road to die.

A Levite came along. He didn't want to help. He stepped over the man and went on his way.

A priest came along. He didn't want to help either. He walked around the injured man and went on his way.

A Samaritan came along. He was from a place far away. Yet, he stopped and helped the man. He took the man to an inn to stay until the man was well.

13
12
2
3
1
11
4
10
5
9
6
8
7

• Love Your Neighbor •

Love Your Neighbor

"Love your neighbor,"

"Love your neighbor,"

Jesus said.

Jesus said.

I can love my neighbor.

I can love my neighbor.

You can too.

You can too.

What You Need
• duplicated page

What to Do
1. Sing the "Love Your Neighbor" song with the class to the tune of "Are You Sleeping?" When you say the word "love," encourage the children to put their hands on their hearts.
2. Teach the children the actions in "I Love You."

I Love You

I

point to self

Love

cross hands over heart

You.

point to another person

■ Loving ■

33

craft

What You Need

• duplicated page
• plastic lids
• yarn
• tape

What to Do

1. Before class, cut out the three hearts for each child. Poke a hole in the center of each lid.
2. Help the children tape the three hearts around a lid so that they hang off the side of the lid.
3. Thread a loop of yarn through the hole and tape to form a hanger.
4. Show the children how to make the hearts spin by twisting the lid and letting go. Say, **Our hearts say, Love your neighbor. God wants us to love everyone.**

■ **Loving** ■

• Heart Spinners •

• Who Is My Neighbor? •

coloring

What You Need
• duplicated page
• crayons

What to Do
1. Hold one copy of the picture so the children can see it as you tell the story.
2. Afterward, while the children color their pictures, ask, **What other ways can we show love to our neighbors?**

Caitlyn helped Mommy place some cans of food in a box. "Who are we taking this food to?" she asked.

Mommy said, "We are taking it to the food pantry. Many people don't have enough food to eat."

"But who will get the food?" Caitlyn asked. "Will it be someone we know?"

Mommy gave Caitlyn some more cans to put into the box. "We may not know the people," she said. "But, they are still our neighbors. Remember the story of the Good Samaritan? He didn't know the man who was hurt. But he helped him anyway. God wants us to love and help everyone."

Caitlyn smiled and put the last can of the food into the box. "I think I'll draw a picture for my neighbors that I don't know. Will you help me write 'I love you,' on the picture?"

Mommy said, "Of course. I think God is pleased with your idea because you are loving someone as He said we should."

■ Loving ■

craft

What You Need
- duplicated page
- large paper lace doilies, any color
- glue

What to Do
1. Before class, cut out a heart for each child.
2. Have the children color their hearts.
3. Help the children glue the heart picture to a paper doily. (For older children, spread some glue inside the letters and then sprinkle glitter or colored sand.)
4. Say, **You can give this heart to someone to tell them you love them.**

■ **Loving** ■

• I Love You Hearts •

I Love You!

Love the Lord...and love your neighbor.
~ Luke 10:27

• Love Heart Jigglers •

snack

What You Need

- duplicated page
- gelatin jigglers (see recipe)
- deep-sided cookie sheet
- heart-shaped cookie cutters
- spatula
- napkins
- washcloths
- small plastic bowls with lids
- tape

What to Do

1. Make the gelatin (see recipe) before class so the gelatin will be set by class time. Make enough so each child can cut two heart shapes from the set gelatin. From this page, cut out a heart for each child.
2. Help the children press a heart cookie cutter into the gelatin.
3. Lift out the heart and place it on a napkin.
4. Say, **The hearts remind us that God wants us to love Him and to love others.**

continued at left

■ Loving ■

Jigglers Recipe

- 2 large or 3 small boxes gelatin
- 2 cups boiling water
- 2 cups cold water

1. Pour gelatin into a mixing bowl.
2. Carefully add boiling water. Stir well.
3. Add cold water and stir.
4. Pour gelatin liquid into a deep-sided cookie sheet.
5. Chill until set.

Love the Lord….and love your neighbor.
~ Luke 10:27

What to Do, continued

5. Let each child make two or three hearts, one to eat and one or two to place in a bowl and take home.
6. To make the heart bowls, help each child tape a heart to a lid.
7. Say, **The heart has our memory verse printed on it. Can you help me say the memory verse?** Repeat the verse several times.

37

Chapter 4

God Wants Me to Be Thankful

Memory Verse

One...came back, praising God.
Luke 17:15

* Story to Share *

2's and 3's ↝

As Jesus was going into a town, 10 men who had leprosy met up with Him. They stood away from Jesus and called out in a loud voice, "Jesus, have pity on us!"

Jesus wanted to make them well. He said, "Go, show yourselves to the priests."

As they left, their leprosy disappeared. They were well!

One of the men, when he saw he was well, came back, praising God.

"Thank You," he said to Jesus.

Jesus asked where the other nine men were. But only one had come back to thank Him.

1's and young 2's ↝

Ten men were sick. When they saw Jesus, they yelled, "Make us well."

Jesus wanted them all to be well. He said, "Go show yourselves to the priests." When they went away, they all became well.

When one of the 10 men saw that he was well, he came back and praised God.

"Thank You," he said to Jesus.

Jesus asked why only one of the 10 men remembered to say, "Thank You."

Based on Luke 17:11-19

Questions for Discussion

1. How many men did Jesus make well?

2. How many men came back and said, "Thank You"?

• Ten Men •

story visual

What You Need
- duplicated page
- scissors

What to Do
1. Fold the page on the dashed lines where indicated.
2. Cut the solid lines to make ten tabs that will fold to the back of the picture.
3. To tell the story, hold the picture with all tabs folded to the back. Bring each one out and count, "one man was sick, two men were sick," etc. Then, bend the tabs back one at a time and count, "one man went away well, two men went away well," etc. Then, bring out the number 1 tab again. Say, **One man came back to thank Jesus.**

Another Idea
Arrange the children in a line. Say, **Sam, you may take two steps forward. Don't forget to say, "Thank you."** Have the children take steps, hop, turn in a circle, etc.

■ **Thankful** ■

bulletin board

· · · · · · · · · · · ·

What You Need

- pattern on page 41
- construction paper or card stock
- clear, self-stick plastic
- praying hands stickers

What to Do

1. Depending on how you want to use the poster (see ideas below and at right), enlarge, reduce or simply copy page 41 to fit your bulletin board space.
2. To use the poster as an in-class activity, duplicate one copy for each child. Have the children color their pictures. Then give the children praying hands stickers to add to the picture.

■ **Thankful** ■

• Bulletin Board Poster •

Poster Pointer

Copy the poster, then copy a letter to parents on the back with classroom updates such as the week's memory verse, a report on the child's good and bad behavior, supply needs and so on.

One...came back, praising God.
Luke 17:15

activity

What You Need
- duplicated page
- crayons
- praying hands stickers

What to Do
1. Give each child a copy of the page.
2. Read the story aloud.
3. Help the children count from one to ten.
4. Say, **How many men came back to thank Jesus? Yes, only ONE came back. God wants us to be thankful like the one man.**
5. Help the children place a sticker on the boxes of things for which they are thankful.

• Thank You •

parents

friends

home

Ten men had leprosy. They couldn't come near anyone while they were sick.

The men saw Jesus and yelled, "Make us well!"

Jesus said, "Go show yourselves to the priests."

When they went away, they were well.

Ten men were made well.

One man turned and came back.

"Thank You, Jesus," he said.

"Where are the other nine?" Jesus asked.

Only one man came back to thank Jesus.

food

church

Jesus

■ **Thankful** ■

42

• Jesus Healed Ten Men •

Thank You, Jesus

Jesus gives us all good things.
He gives all we need.
He takes good care of you and me.
THANK YOU, JESUS!

What You Need
• duplicated page

Jesus Healed Ten Men

One, two, three,
Four, five, six
Seven, eight, nine,
And TEN.
Jesus made ten men well.

Ten, nine, eight,
Seven, six, five,
Four, three, two,
And ONE.
Only one
man said,
"Thank You."

What to Do

1. Practice the "Jesus Healed Ten Men" counting story before class. Hold up your fingers to count as you tell the story. Help the children to hold up their fingers to count, too.

2. Sit down to sing the song, "Thank You, Jesus."

3. Sing the song to the tune of "Pop Goes the Weasel" in a normal voice until you get to the last line, then sing the last line and jump up. Repeat several times with the children.

■ **Thankful** ■

43

craft

What You Need
• duplicated page
• crayons

What to Do
1. Before class, cut out a praying hands figure for each child.
2. Help the children fold their praying hands with the words on the inside.
3. While the children color their crafts, say, **Let's name some things for which we can thank Jesus. I can thank Jesus for a church where I can learn about Him.** Allow the children to share their own ideas for thanks.

■ **Thankful** ■

• Praying Hands •

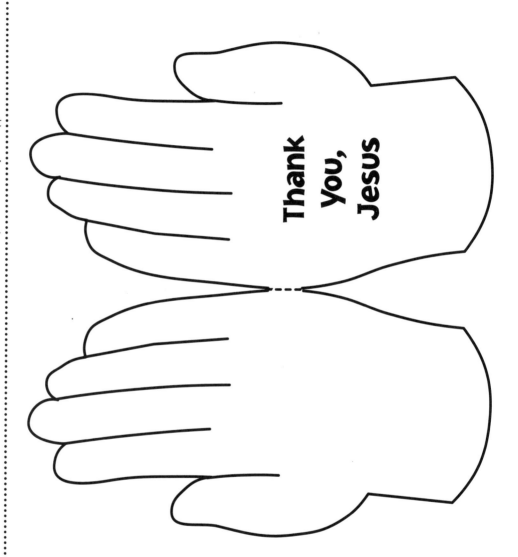

Thank You, Jesus

• Remembering to Pray •

coloring

What You Need
- duplicated page
- crayons

What to Do
1. Hold up a copy of the picture so all the children can see it as you tell the story.
2. Give each child a copy of the page to color.

Zack grabbed a handful of potato chips and began to eat them. "These are good," he said. "Give me some more."

Amy held the bag away from him. "You didn't say, 'Thank you.'"

"Oh, yeah," Zack said. "I forgot. Thank you."

Amy still held the bag away from Zack. "No," she said. "You didn't thank Jesus."

Zack bowed his head as he prayed, "Thank You, for these potato chips and for all the good things You give us."

Amy held out the bag for Zack. He grabbed the bag. "I didn't hear YOU pray," he said.

Amy prayed, too. Then, they both enjoyed the potato chips.

■ Thankful ■

45

game

What You Need

- duplicated page
- card stock (white or colored)
- tape

What to Do

1. Before class, cut out the block shape.
2. Fold it on the dashed lines to form a block, and tape the seams.
3. Have the children take turns tossing the block onto the table.
4. Say the name of the picture that is on top. Say, **The block has a dog on top. Let's thank God for our pets.**
5. Have the children thank God.
6. For older children, make two blocks and play a matching/toss game. The children should throw both blocks and try to have the top pictures match.

■ **Thankful** ■

• Thank You Block •

• Thank You Treats •

snack

What You Need
- duplicated page
- small candy
- envelopes

What to Do
1. Give each child a copy of the duplicated page and some candy.
2. Help the children trace the letters with their candy to spell THANK YOU.
3. Lead the class in a short prayer. Encourage the children to take turns saying, "Thank You" during the prayer.
4. Allow the children to eat some of the candy. (Do not give young children hard candy that could be a choking hazard.)
5. Fold the page and put it, with some candies, into an envelope for the children to take home.

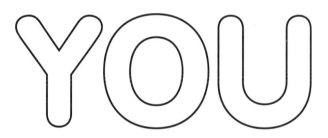

One…came back, praising God.
~ Luke 17:15

■ Thankful ■

47

Chapter 5

God Wants Me to Share

Memory Verse

They shared everything they had.
Acts 4:32

* Story to Share *

2's and 3's

After Jesus went to heaven, the church began. The people in the first church liked to share with each other. No one thought that their things were only their own. Everyone shared everything they had.

People in the church gave to help others, and they even sold land or houses and brought the money to the apostles. The apostles used the money to help anyone who needed it.

1's and young 2's

The church began after Jesus went to heaven. All the people in the church shared everything. Whatever they had, they gave to help each other.

Some people even sold their houses and their land. They brought the money to the church to help others.

Based on Acts 4:32-37

Questions for Discussion

1. What began after Jesus went to heaven?
2. What did some people sell so they could give money to help the church?

• Story-go-round •

story visual
. . . .

What You Need
- duplicated page
- tape

What to Do
1. Color the strips and cut them apart lengthwise on the solid lines.
2. Tape the two strips together in a circle.
3. Move the story-go-round in a circle as you tell the story. Allow the children to see all the pictures of the people sharing.

Another Idea
Arrange the children in a circle. Give each child a toy (bear, doll, truck, etc.) Play some music. When the music stops, the children should pass their toy to the person on their right. Repeat several times. Say, **It doesn't matter what we have. We can share all that we have with others. God wants us to be people who share.**

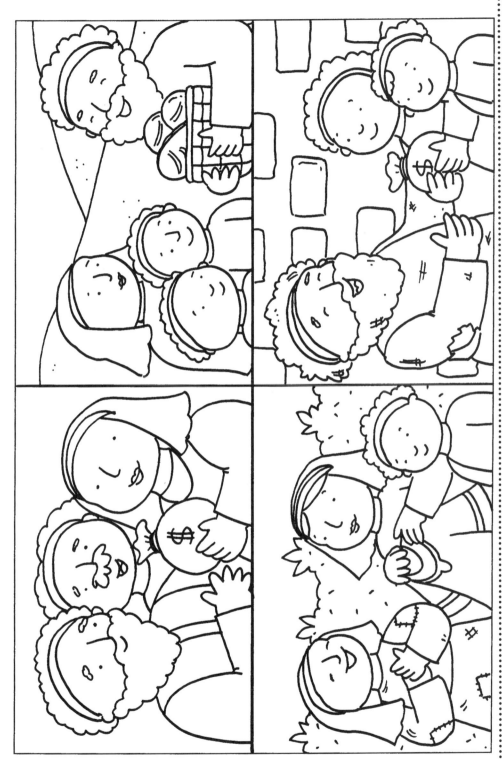

■ **Share** ■

bulletin board

. . . .

What You Need

- pattern on page 51
- construction paper or card stock
- clear, self-stick plastic
- play money
- glue

What to Do

1. Depending on how you want to use the poster (see ideas below and at right), enlarge, reduce or simply copy page 51 to fit your bulletin board space.

2. To use the poster as an in-class activity, copy the poster for each child. Give each child one or two play dollar bills to glue onto the back of the poster. Say, **We can give our money to help others. What other things can we give? Yes, we can give food. Yes, we can give clothes.** (And so on.) **God wants us to share.**

■ **Share** ■

• Bulletin Board Poster •

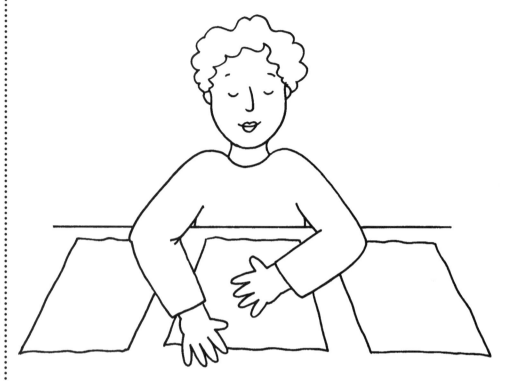

Poster Pointer

Copy the poster and tape several onto a table. Cover the table with removable clear plastic and provide crayons for a before class coloring activity. Wipe off crayon marks with a damp cloth after class to provide a clean surface for the following week.

They shared everything they had.
Acts 4:32

puzzle

. . . .

What You Need

• duplicated page
• crayons

What to Do

1. Help the children draw a line from each picture to the apostles in the center of the page.

2. Say, **These people are bringing money to help others. The early church shared everything they had. The people brought many things to share with others. Some brought food, some brought clothes, others brought money. Even the children had things to share. God wants us to share.**

■ **Share** ■

• Bringing Something to Help •

• God Wants Me to Share •

God Wants Me to Share

God wants me to share,

God wants me to share,

I will share with others,

God wants me to share.

I can share my food,

I can share my food,

I will share with others,

I can share my food.

I can share my toys,

I can share my toys,

I will share with others,

I can share my toys.

God wants me to share,

God wants me to share,

I will share with others,

God wants me to share.

song

What You Need
• duplicated page

What to Do
1. Sing "God Wants Me to Share" with the children to the tune of "The Farmer in the Dell."
2. When you sing the word "share," encourage the children to hold out their hands.

■ Share ■

craft

What You Need
• duplicated page
• paper plates
• glue
• yarn
• crayons

What to Do
1. Before class, cut out the four handprints for each child.
2. Write the memory verse from page 48 in the center of each plate.
3. Help the children arrange the handprints onto the rim of the plate.
4. Glue the handprints into place.
5. Add a loop of yarn for a hanger.
6. Have the children color their wreaths.

■ **Share** ■

• Sharing Wreath •

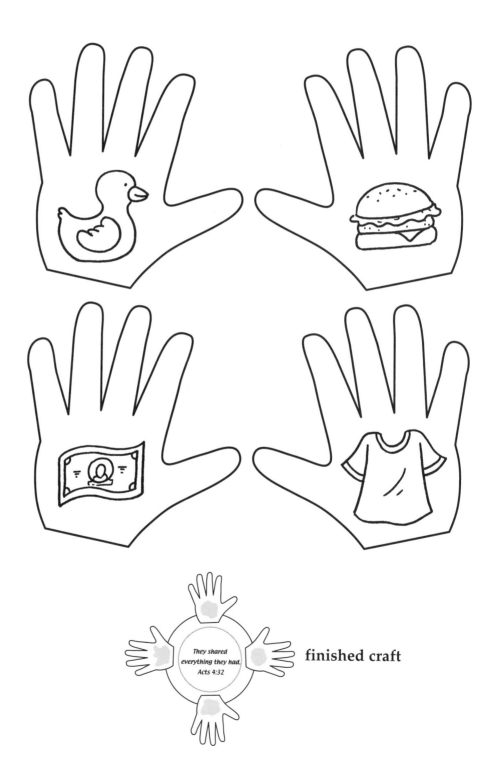

They shared everything they had. Acts 4:32

finished craft

• Sharing Coupon •

will remember to share.

They shared everything they had. ~ Acts 4:32

activity

What You Need
- duplicated page
- crayons

What to Do
1. Hold a copy of the page so that all the children can see it as you read the story.
2. Allow the children to color the coupon after you finish the story.
3. Cut out the coupon for each child to take home as a reminder to share.

"I don't want to play with David," Jenna said. "He wants to play with all my toys."

"Jenna," Mom said. "Don't you remember what you learned in Sunday school?"

Jenna's mom was the Sunday school teacher. Jenna liked to listen to her Mom teach Bible lessons.

"I remember," Jenna said. "The people in the early church shared everything they had. I guess I should share what I have with David. But he doesn't want to share with me when he brings a toy."

Mom shook her head. "I have an idea," she said. "Let's make a coupon to give to David. Maybe you both will remember to share."

Mom got out a piece of paper. Jenna drew a picture of toys. Mom wrote on the paper, SHARING COUPON. Then she helped Jenna write her name on the line.

When David came over to play, Jenna gave him the coupon. "This is to remind me to share with you," Jenna said.

David showed Jenna the airplane he brought. "I will remember to share with you, too," he said.

■ Share ■

55

craft

What You Need

- duplicated page
- glue
- pictures of toys, food, clothing
- plain paper
- tape

What to Do

1. Before class, cut out one caterpillar face for each child and use the circle to trace and cut several circles from plain paper for each child. Tear pages from old magazines that have pictures of items children should share.
2. Help the children glue the pictures of things to share onto the plain circles.
3. Make a caterpillar for each child by taping all of the circles in a row behind the face.

• Sharing Caterpillar •

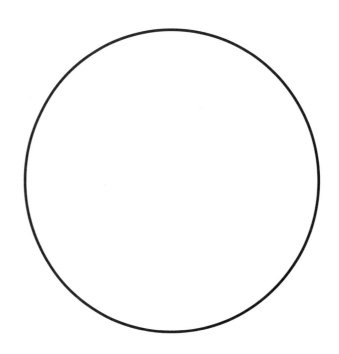

■ **Share** ■

• Popcorn Bags •

It's fun to share!
Acts 4:32-37

It's fun to share!
Acts 4:32-37

It's fun to share!
Acts 4:32-37

snack

What You Need
- duplicated page
- paper lunch sacks
- popcorn
- tape

What to Do
1. Before class, prepare the popcorn. Cut out a smiley face for each child (each page includes a face for three children).
2. Help the children tape a smiley face to a paper sack.
3. Help the children put some popcorn in their bags.
4. Take the children to another class to give away their popcorn bags. Make sure there are enough bags to share with everyone in the class you visit.
5. Say, **God wants us to share. It's fun to share with others.**

■ Share ■

Chapter 6

God Wants Me to Be Healthy

Memory Verse

You...are God's temple.
1 Corinthians 3:16

* Story to Share *

2's and 3's ⟶

Daniel and three friends were among the young men chosen to serve in the king's palace. The men were to be trained for three years. Then they would serve the king.

The king wanted them to eat the same kind of food he ate each day.

"No," Daniel said. Daniel knew God only wanted him to eat healthy food, but the king's food was not healthy. He asked to be able to eat only vegetables and to drink only water.

The chief official was afraid of the king. He didn't want the king to see Daniel and his three friends looking thin. So he told them they would have to eat the food the king had ordered them to eat.

"No!" Daniel said, "Let's have a test. We will eat only vegetables and drink only water for ten days. At the end of that time, if we don't look healthy, then we will eat what the king has ordered.

At the end of the ten days, the chief official was surprised. Daniel and his three friends looked healthier than any of the other young men. Daniel was right: the king's food wasn't good for them. God wanted them to eat healthy food.

1's and young 2's ⟶

Daniel and his three friends were learning to be servants in the king's palace. The king wanted them to learn many things. He wanted them to eat only unhealthy food, just like he did.

"No, no," Daniel said. "We shouldn't eat that kind of food. No, that food isn't good for us."

A chief told Daniel he would have to eat the king's food. "No," Daniel said. "Give us vegetables and water for ten days and you will see. God wants us to be healthy."

After ten days, Daniel and his three friends were healthier than all the other young men. So, the chief let them eat and drink what they wanted.

Based on Daniel 1

❓ Questions for Discussion

1. What did Daniel and his three friends want to eat and drink?

2. What happened when they ate only vegetables and drank only water?

• Shaking Head Daniel •

story visual
· · · · · · · · · · · · ·

What You Need
- duplicated page
- paper lunch sack
- glue

What to Do
1. Cut out the patterns and color them.
2. Turn the paper bag upside down, so the open edge is at the bottom.
3. Glue the front of Daniel's face to one side of the bag, about five inches up from the opened edge.
4. Glue the back of Daniel's head to the other side of the bag in the same area.
5. To tell the story, slip the puppet over your hand. Move the puppet when Daniel is talking. Shake the head loosely on your hand so that it moves back and forth as if to say, "No" when Daniel is talking about not eating the king's food.

■ **Healthy** ■

59

bulletin board

· · · · · · · · · · · ·

What You Need
- pattern on page 61
- construction paper or card stock
- clear, self-stick plastic
- glue
- CDs
- ribbon

What to Do
1. Depending on how you want to use the poster (see ideas below and at right), enlarge, reduce or simply copy page 61 to fit your bulletin board space.
2. To use the poster as an in-class activity, make a mirror plaque. Provide a copy of the poster for each child. Turn a sheet of construction paper sideways. Glue the poster to the right edge of the paper. On the left side, tape a computer CD, with the mirrored side out. Add a length of ribbon to the top for a hanger. Say, **You can look at yourself to remember that God wants you to be healthy.**

■ Healthy ■

• Bulletin Board Poster •

Poster Pointer

Copy each poster to card stock, one for each child. Punch holes in eight or 10 places around the edge of the card. Put a small piece of tape around the end of a one-yard length of yarn for easy lacing. Let the children lace the cards. Say the memory verse several times while the children are working and encourage them to say it with you.

You...are God's temple.

1 Corinthians 3:16

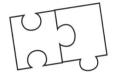

puzzle

What You Need
- duplicated page
- crayons

What to Do
1. Read the story again to the children from page 58.
2. Have the children find three carrots, three apples, two stalks of broccoli and one bunch of grapes in the picture. They should color them the appropriate colors.

• Hidden Veggies •

■ Healthy ■

• Eat Good Food •

Eat Good Food

Eat good food.

Eat good food.   *pretend to eat*

That's what God wants us to do.

point to God

If we want to grow up strong and good.

flex muscles

Then we must only eat good food.

pretend to eat

Growing Song

I am growing stronger.
I am growing stronger.
I am growing stronger.
Just see what I can do.

I am eating good food.
I am eating good food.
I am eating good food.
Just see what I can do.

My body is God's temple.
My body is God's temple.
My body is God's temple.
Just see what I can do.

song

What You Need
• duplicated page

What to Do
1. Practice singing "Eat Good Food" to the tune of "This Old Man" using the actions. Sing the song with the children and help them learn the actions. Repeat several times.
2. Sing the "Growing Song" with the children to the tune of "The Bear Went Over the Mountain." To add actions, pretend to grow taller as you sing the verses.

■ **Healthy** ■

craft

What You Need
- duplicated page
- crayons
- ribbon
- tape

What to Do
1. Before class, cut out the three panels for each child.
2. Allow time for the children to color the pictures.
3. Help the children tape the panels to a length of ribbon. They can choose which picture to put at the top, middle and bottom of the banner.
4. While the children color their posters, read each panel to them. Say, **We eat well to take care of ourselves. We need plenty of rest to take care of ourselves. We should take care of our bodies. God wants us to be healthy.**

■ Healthy ■

• I Will Take Care of My Body •

• I Can Take Care of Myself •

coloring

What You Need
• duplicated page
• crayons

What to Do
1. Show the children a copy of the picture as you read the story to them.
2. Ask, **What things can you do to take care of yourself? God wants us to be healthy.**

"**I** have a new toothbrush," Dylan told Dad. "The dentist said I have good teeth, but I need to brush them to take care of them."

"Good," Dad said. "You are big enough to take care of your teeth. You are getting bigger each day."

"I can brush my own hair and wash my face," Dylan said. "And I like to eat my vegetables."

Dad gave Dylan a big hug. "You are growing up so fast! I am glad you are taking good care of yourself. God wants us to take good care of the bodies He has given us."

▪ Healthy ▪

craft

What You Need
- duplicated page
- small powdered drink mix containers
- tape
- clear, self-stick plastic
- crayons

What to Do

1. Before class, cut out the panel on the page for each child. Cut a 1" x 2" hole in the top of each plastic lid. (The containers should be about the size of a 12-oz frozen juice can.)
2. Have the children color the label.
3. Tape the label around the plastic can.
4. Help the children wrap clear, self-stick plastic over the entire panel to make it waterproof.
5. Put the lid on the can.
6. Say, **We can use our toothbrush holders to put toothbrushes in. God likes when we brush our teeth and take care of bodies. He wants us to be healthy.**

■ Healthy ■

• Toothbrush Holder •

I Take Good Care Of Me!

You...are God's temple. ~ 1 Corinthians 3:16

• Toss and Catch •
Paper Beanbag

God wants me to be healthy!

game

What You Need
- duplicated page
- paper
- tape

What to Do
1. Before class, cut the rectangle from the page. Fold the rectangle on the dashed line. Tape two of the open sides. Stuff the "beanbag" with wadded paper. Tape the remaining side closed. Make at least one bag for every three students.
2. Divide the children into groups of three. Have an adult helper for each group.
3. Toss the beanbag to a child. Have the child toss the beanbag back to you. Then toss it to another child.
4. Say, **We are having fun while we are exercising. God wants us to exercise and be healthy.**

■ Healthy ■

Chapter 7

God Wants Me to Be Obedient

Memory Verse

I give him to the Lord. 1 Samuel 1:28

* Story to Share *

2's and 3's

Hannah wanted a son. She prayed and prayed for God to give her a son. One day, at the temple, she cried as she prayed, "God, if You will give me a son of my own, I will give him back to You to work in the temple."

Eli, the priest, saw her praying. "I pray that God will bless you with what you want," he said.

Soon, Hannah had a son. She named him Samuel. Hannah was very happy that God answered her prayers for a son. "I will remember my promise," she said.

When Samuel was not a baby anymore, Hannah took him to the temple. She said to Eli, "I promised God I would give my son to Him. I promised that Samuel would work for God in the temple. Here is my son."

Hannah left Samuel at the temple to work for God. Samuel obeyed his mother and stayed at the temple. Samuel obeyed Eli in the temple. Samuel obeyed God.

1's and young 2's

Hannah prayed for a baby boy. She prayed a long time.

One day, she promised God that if He gave her a son she would take her son to work in the temple.

Hannah soon had a baby boy named Samuel. When he grew up, Hannah took Samuel to work at the temple. Hannah said, "I am keeping my promise. Here is my son to work in the temple."

Samuel obeyed his mother. Samuel obeyed Eli in the temple. Samuel obeyed God.

Based on 1 Samuel 1; 2:18-21

Questions for Discussion

1. For what did Hannah ask God?

2. What was her promise to God?

3. Where did she take Samuel when he was no longer a baby?

• Story Stand-ups •

story visual

What You Need
• duplicated page

What to Do
1. Color the pictures and cut the Stand-ups from the page.
2. Fold each Stand-up at the dashed lines, so it will stand up.
3. Move the three figures around as you tell the story. Each Stand-up has two pictures of the character.

More Ideas
1. Plan an easy task for the children to do in the church, such as handing out bulletins. Say, **Samuel obeyed and helped in the temple. We can obey God by helping in our church.**
2. Make a set of Story Stand-ups from card stock for each child. While the children play with them, say, **This is Hannah praying for a son. This is Samuel obeying and serving the Lord.** And so on.

▪ Obedient ▪

bulletin board

· · · · · · · · · · · ·

What You Need

- pattern on page 71
- construction paper or card stock
- clear, self-stick plastic
- crayons

What to Do

1. Depending on how you want to use the poster (see ideas below and at right), enlarge, reduce or simply copy page 71 to fit your bulletin board space.

2. To use the poster as an in-class activity, duplicate one copy for each child. Cut inward at the dots and around the top of the temple. Fold the top part of the picture behind so the picture will stand. Have the children color their pictures, then show them how to make the pop-up picture stand.

■ **Obedient** ■

• Bulletin Board Poster •

Poster Pointer

Make one or more copies of the unit poster book (see instructions on page 89). Keep the books visible for children to "read."

I give him to the Lord.

1 Samuel 1:28

puzzle

What You Need
• duplicated page
• crayons

What to Do
1. Give each child a copy of the page.
2. Say, **This is Hannah keeping her promise to God. Samuel obeyed his mother and Eli, and he obeyed God.**
3. Help the children find and color the happy faces in the picture as you read the story from page 68. Say, **God is happy when we obey Him. We should be happy to do good things for God.**
4. Allow the children to color the picture of Hannah and Samuel.

■ Obedient ■

• Happy to Obey •

Holy Temple

• I Obey •

Obey

Samuel served and obeyed God,
Obeyed God,
Obeyed God.
Samuel served and obeyed God.
God wants us to obey.

I will obey Mom and Dad,
Mom and Dad,
Mom and Dad.
I will obey Mom and Dad.
God wants me to obey.

I will obey God above,
God above,
God above.
I will obey God above.
God wants me to obey.

Holy Temple

pretend to pick up toys

pretend to eat

I Will Obey

When Mom says, "Let's pick up toys,"
I will obey.

When Mom says, "Please eat your food,"
I will obey.

When Mom says, "It's time for bed,"
I will obey.

pretend to sleep

craft

What You Need
• duplicated page
• paper grocery bags
• glue
• crayons

What to Do
1. Before class, cut out four "Be Good" patches for each child. Cut a vest from a paper bag for each child (see illustration).
2. Allow the children to color the patches.
3. Help the children glue the patches to the fronts of their vests.
4. Say, **When we wear our Be Good Vests, we will remember to obey God and our parents. God wants us to be good.**

■ **Obedient** ■

• Be Good for God Vest •

I can be good for God.

I will obey God.

I will obey my parents.

God wants me to obey.

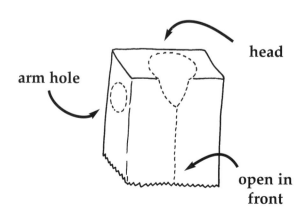

head

arm hole

open in front

• Tiffany Obeys •

coloring

What You Need
- duplicated page
- crayons

What to Do
1. Hold up one copy of the page so all the children can see it as you tell the story.
2. Afterward, give each child a copy of the page to color.
3. Ask, **In what other ways can we obey? God wants us to be obedient.**

Tiffany looked around her room for her shoes. "Here is one shoe," she said. She picked up a shoe from under a pile of clothes. Then, she began to search for the other shoe.

"What a mess!" Mom said. "Your room looks awful. Please pick up your things and put them away."

Mom left the room. Tiffany searched for her other shoe. Then she went to the living room to watch TV.

Later, Mom came from Tiffany's room. "You didn't clean up your room. You didn't obey me."

Tiffany frowned. "We had a story in Sunday school about Samuel. He obeyed his mommy. He went to the temple to serve God. I am sorry I didn't pick up my things."

Tiffany went to her room and cleaned up the mess. She put all her toys away. She put her dirty clothes in the basket. She placed her favorite teddy bear on the bed. "There," she said. "I obeyed. I am sorry I didn't obey at first."

Mom came into the room and gave Tiffany a hug. "You did a wonderful job. Thank you for obeying."

■ **Obedient** ■

craft

What You Need
- duplicated page
- plastic drinking straws
- crayons
- scissors
- tape
- paper cups
- glue sticks (optional)
- colored sugar (optional)

What to Do
1. Before class, cut out the three flowers for each child.
2. Have the children color their flowers. If desired, allow the children to use a glue stick to glue colored sugar on the flowers.
3. Help the children tape each flower onto a straw.
4. Show how to place the flowers in a paper cup to carry home.
5. Say, **The flowers say, "I will obey, Mom." "I will obey Dad." "I will obey God." In what ways can we obey?**

■ Obedient ■

• Obey Bouquet •

• Dedicated to God •

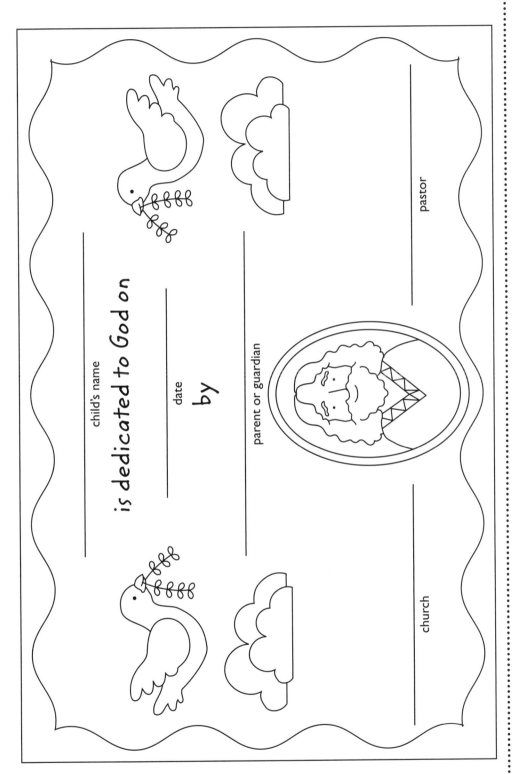

child's name

is dedicated to God on

date

by

parent or guardian

pastor

church

activity

What You Need
- duplicated page
- Bibles

What to Do
1. Hold a dedication ceremony, either in your classroom or in the church sanctuary. You may make this ceremony as large or small as you wish.
2. Recognize each child and his or her parents.
3. Give each child a copy of the certificate.
4. Say, **Samuel's mother dedicated him to serve God. Now, Bobby, your parents will dedicate you to God. You are a child of God. We are proud to have you as part of our church** (class, nursery).
5. If desired, present each child with a small Bible or testament in addition to the certificate.

■ Obedient ■

Chapter 8

God Wants Me to Be a Good Friend

Memory Verse

Where you go I will go...your God [will be] my God. Ruth 1:16

* Story to Share *

2's and 3's ⟿

Naomi and her husband had two sons. They moved far away from home because they needed to find food.

After a few years, Naomi's husband died. One of Naomi's sons married Orpah and the other married Ruth. After 10 years, the sons died also.

Naomi wanted to go back to her family in Judah. She told Orpah and Ruth to go back to their own families and find new husbands. But Ruth loved Naomi. She didn't want to leave Naomi alone.

Ruth went with Naomi back to Judah. She said, "Where you go I will go. Your God will be my God." Ruth was a good friend to Naomi. She helped in the fields to get food for Naomi. God blessed Ruth for being a good friend.

1's and young 2's ⟿

Naomi needed a friend. Her husband had died. Her sons had died. She wanted to go back to her family's country and start a new life. But Ruth wouldn't let her go alone.

"I will help take care of you," Ruth said. "Where you go, I will go. Your God will be my God."

Ruth went with Naomi and was a good friend. She helped get food for Naomi. God blessed Ruth for being a good friend.

Based on Ruth 1

Questions for Discussion

1. Who was a good friend to Naomi?

2. How did Ruth help Naomi?

• Heart to Heart Friends •

story visual

What You Need
- duplicated page
- construction paper
- glue

What to Do
1. Color and cut out the two women figures from the page.
2. Cut a large heart shape from construction paper.
3. Glue one of the women figures to each side of the heart.
4. To tell the story, show each side of the heart as the woman is mentioned.
5. Say, **A heart means love. We love our friends. Ruth loved her friend Naomi and helped her. Ruth was a good friend.**

Another Idea
Duplicate and cut out the figures for each child. Help the children glue each figure onto a separate paper lunch sack and slip both puppets over their hands to pretend to be Naomi and Ruth. Say, **Ruth was a good friend to Naomi.**

■ Friend ■

bulletin board

What You Need
- pattern on page 81
- construction paper or card stock
- clear, self-stick plastic
- washable paint

What to Do
1. Depending on how you want to use the poster (see ideas below and at right), enlarge, reduce or simply copy page 81 to fit your bulletin board space.
2. To use the poster as an in-class activity, duplicate a copy for each child. Help the children press a handprint of washable paint onto the page. Say, **Good friends give each other a hand to be helpful. How can you help your friends?**

■ **Friend** ■

• Bulletin Board Poster •

Poster Pointer

Tape a plastic page protector outside your classroom door. Above the page protector, place a sign that reads "This is what we are learning today." Slip the colored poster for the week into the page protector. Parents will know what their children are learning, and toddlers will be excited to see the new poster each week.

Where you go I will go...your God will be my God.
Ruth 1:16

activity

What You Need
- duplicated page
- crayons

What to Do
1. Give each child a copy of the page.
2. Read the story to the children from page 78.
3. Say, **Naomi and Ruth were good friends because they obeyed God. Do good friends have happy or sad faces?**
4. Help the children draw happy faces on Naomi and Ruth.

■ **Friend** ■

• Good Friends •

• Wherever You Go •

Wherever You Go

Ruth told Naomi, "I am your friend,
And I'll go where you go."
"Wherever you will go,
Wherever you will go,
Wherever you will go,
I will go there, too."

Good Friend

Good friend.
Good friend.
I can be a good friend.
I can help my friends.

Good friend.
Good friend.
I can be a good friend.
I'll share with my friends.

Good friend.
Good friend.
I can be a good friend.
I will love my friends.

song/verse

. . . .

What You Need

• duplicated page

What to Do

1. Sing "Wherever You Go" with the children to the tune of "B-I-N-G-O." Then have the children hold hands with a friend and sing the song again.
2. Say the "Good Friend" verse with the children. Tell them to clasp their hands together (show them how) every time they hear the word "friend."

■ Friend ■

craft

What You Need
• duplicated page
• crayons
• stapler
• tape

What to Do

1. Before class, cut the page apart into four sections and place the pictures in order from 1 to 4. Staple the booklet at the left edge. Cover the staples with tape to avoid injury.

2. Have the children color the pictures in their booklets.

3. As the children turn the pages together, say, **Good friends help. Good friends share. Good friends love each other. God wants us to be good friends.**

■ **Friend** ■

• Good Friends Booklet •

Good friends.   1

Good friends help.   2

Good friends
share.   3

Good friends
love each other.
(Ruth 1:16)   4

• Friends Pray •

coloring

What You Need
- duplicated page
- crayons

What to Do
1. Give a copy of the page to each child.
2. Read the story to the children while they color their pictures.

Jon sat in church with Daddy. Mommy was in the hospital. Jon was afraid because Mommy was very sick.

Someone tapped Jon on the shoulder. He turned in the pew to see Abby and her mom. "Would you and your dad like to come for lunch at our house?" Abby asked.

Jon looked at his dad. Daddy said, "Well, I would like to go straight to the hospital after church, but Jon could sure use a friend right now."

Jon went home with Abby and her mom. They had a good lunch of chicken and potatoes. "My mom makes really good chicken, too," Jon said.

Abby's mom nodded. "I think this would be a good time for us to pray for your mommy. Good friends pray for each other."

Jon loved being at Abby's house. They played all afternoon. Jon wasn't afraid anymore. He was glad to have good friends.

85

■ Friend ■

craft

What You Need
- duplicated page
- crayons
- white paper
- stapler
- tape

What to Do
1. Before class, cut out a crown for each child. Cut a 1" x 8" strip of paper for each child.
2. Have the children color their crowns.
3. Fasten on the crowns by stapling a strip of paper to one end, then fitting the other end and stapling to the crown. (Cover the staples with tape to avoid injury.)
4. Say, **Our crowns will remind us that God wants us to be good friends.**

■ **Friend** ■

• Good Friends Crowns •

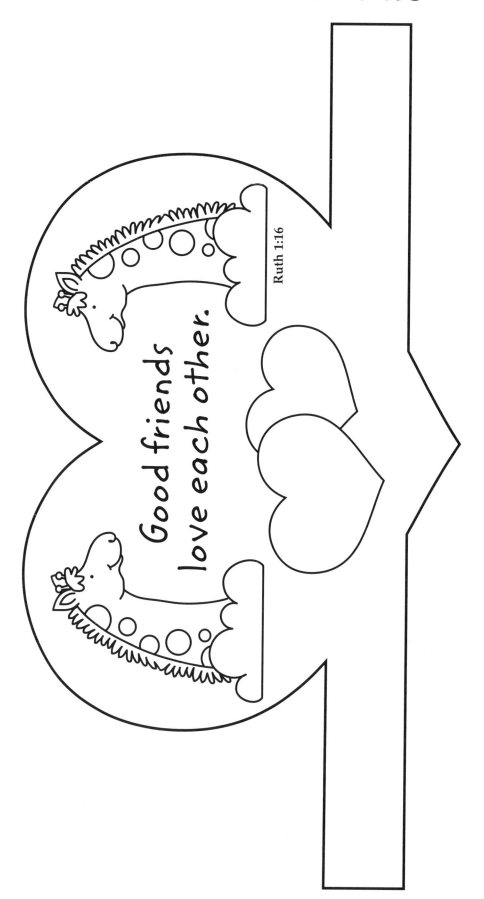

Ruth 1:16

Good friends love each other.

• Good Friends Parade •

I AM A GOOD FRIEND!

I AM A GOOD FRIEND!

game

What You Need
- duplicated page
- several colors of paper
- tape or CD player
- children's tape or CD

What to Do
1. Before class, copy and cut out the friends from colored paper. Be sure you have one set of friends in each paper color.
2. Place the cut-out friends into a bag.
3. Have the children reach into the bag and draw a friend.
4. Have each child pair with the child who has the same color of friend.
5. Say, **Sam has a blue friend. So does Jillian. You can be friends in our "good friends" parade. God wants us to be good friends.**
6. After all the children are paired, play music and have the children parade around the room in pairs.
7. If time allows, repeat the parade with new friends.

■ Friend ■

Chapter 9
More Ways to Grow for God

I Can Be

Sing to the tune of "The Wise Man Built His House Upon the Rock"

I can be what God wants me to be.
I can be what God wants me to be.
I can be what God wants me to be.
It says so in God's Word.

Add these lines:

I can be kind like God wants me to be.

I can be helpful like God wants me to be.

I can be loving like God wants me to be.

I can be thankful like God wants me to be.

I can share like God wants me to share.

I can be healthy like God wants me to be.

I can be obedient like God wants me to be.

I can be a good friend like God wants me to be.

Sing to the tune of "I'm Bringing Home a Baby Bumble Bee":

I can be just what God wants me to be.
Won't my mommy be so proud of me?
I can be just what God wants me to be.
Yes, I CAN BE!

Repeat, substituting these words for "mommy": daddy, grandma, grandpa, teacher, Jesus.

• Growing Up for God Book •

craft

What You Need
- this page and pp. 10, 21, 31, 41, 51, 61, 71 and 81, duplicated
- stapler
- tape

What to Do
1. Help the children arrange the pages as they desire, with this cover page on top of the book.
2. Staple at the left edge. (Cover the staples with tape to avoid injury.)
3. Have the children color in their books if time allows.

I'm Growing Up for God

■ More ■

craft

What You Need
• duplicated page
• crayons

What to Do
1. Before class, cut out the bee pattern for each child. Cut the slits in the bee.
2. Have the children color their bees.
3. Show the children how to slip a hand through the slits and make the bees fly.
4. Say, **The bees remind us to BEE what God wants us to be.**

■ **More** ■

• Bee What God Wants •

I WILL GROW UP TO BEE

WHAT GOD WANTS ME TO BEE

cut

• Best I Can Be Pendant •

I know what God wants for me.

He wants me to be the best I can be!

craft

What You Need
- duplicated page
- crepe paper
- crayons
- tape

What to Do
1. Before class, cut out a figure for each child.
2. Give each child a figure to color.
3. Help the children tape the figure to a length of crepe paper that is about two feet long.
4. Attach the loose ends of the crepe paper with tape.
5. Place the pendants around the children's necks.

■ **More** ■

teacher help
· · · · · · · · · · · · ·

What You Need
- duplicated page
- two sheets of black construction paper
- tape
- bulletin board posters from pp. 10, 21, 31, 41, 51, 61, 71, 81, duplicated
- paper clip
- glue

What to Do
1. Lay the two sheets of construction paper side by side and tape them together at the center.
2. Fold to close like a book.
3. Cut out the HOLY BIBLE label and glue it to the top sheet of construction paper.
4. Each week as you review the memory verse, place the poster for that lesson inside the construction paper Bible. Use a paper clip to hold the poster in place. Open this "Bible" and read the memory verse.

■ More ■

The Holy Bible

• Friends Finger Puppet •

craft

What You Need
- duplicated page
- tape
- crayons

What to Do
1. Before class, cut out the two finger puppets for each child.
2. Have the children color their two puppets.
3. Help the children bend the tabs and tape at the back to form finger puppets.
4. Show how to put the puppets on their fingers.
5. Say, **Show how your friend puppets can tell each other about God.**

I AM GROWING UP FOR GOD.

I AM GROWING UP FOR GOD.

■ **More** ■

game

What You Need
• duplicated page
• music tape or CD
• cassette or CD player

What to Do
1. Make several copies of the happy face. Tape the pages to the floor.
2. Arrange the children in a circle.
3. As the children walk in a circle, play the music.
4. Stop the music periodically.
5. When the music stops, check to see who is standing on a happy face paper.
5. Say, **Ryan and Sara are standing on the happy faces. They both are happy to be what God wants them to be.**

■ **More** ■

• Happy to Be Me •

• Hands and Feet for God •

craft

. . . .

What You Need

- this page and page 96, duplicated
- construction paper
- glue

What to Do

1. Before class, cut out a child shape, hands and feet for each child.
2. Help the children tape the hands and feet to the body.
3. Say, **We can use our hands and feet for God.**

I AM GROWING UP FOR GOD!

■ **More** ■